LIVING
IN HIS
PRESENCE

LIVING
IN HIS
PRESENCE

ROBERT MORRIS

STUDY GUIDE

Living in His Presence Study Guide
Copyright © 2018 by Robert Morris

Content taken from sermons delivered in 2016 by Robert Morris at Gateway Church, Southlake, TX.

ISBN: 978-1-945529-55-9

We hope you hear from the Holy Spirit and receive God's richest blessings from this book by Gateway Press. We want to provide the highest quality resources that take the messages, music, and media of Gateway Church to the world. For more information on other resources from Gateway Publishing, go to gatewaypublishing.com.

Gateway Press, an imprint of Gateway Publishing
700 Blessed Way
Southlake, Texas 76092
gatewaypublishing.com

18 19 20 21 22   7 6 5 4 3 2 1
Printed in the United States of America

CONTENTS

1

HIS PRESENCE

*God is omnipresent—He is everywhere. We can never hide from Him,
but as believers, we can choose to experience His manifest presence by
spending time with Him and listening to His voice every day.*

ENGAGE

What is your favorite sport and/or favorite sports team?

WATCH

Watch "His Presence."

- Think about the world around you and how God is present in it.
- Watch for the different types of God's presence, especially
  His manifest presence.

(If you are not able to watch this teaching on video, read the
following. Otherwise, skip to the **Talk** section after viewing.)

READ

There are three types of God's presence—His omnipresence, His inner presence, and His manifest presence. Omnipresence means God is everywhere, as seen in Psalm 139:7:

> Where can I go from Your Spirit?
> Or where can I flee from Your presence?

There is also the inner presence of God that occurs when Holy Spirit comes and lives inside of us after we get saved.

The third type is the *manifest presence* of God: when He makes His presence known among us. Worship is important to making God's presence known. We realize His presence during worship services, but we can also experience the presence of God every day.

His Manifest Presence

God began His relationship with mankind by walking and talking with Adam and Eve in the Garden of Eden. What did we lose when they fell? And what did Jesus come to restore? His manifest presence.

> And they heard the sound of the Lord God walking in the garden in the cool of the day, and Adam and his wife hid themselves from the presence of the Lord God among the trees of the garden (Genesis 3:8).

Sin always causes us to try to hide from the presence of God— even in a worship service. If you messed up in the past week, Satan will say you shouldn't worship because you will be a hypocrite; however, this is precisely when you need to enter the presence of God. You can enter His presence boldly, even when you make a mistake, because of the blood of Jesus.

Genesis 3:8 can't be talking about God's omnipresence. Since God is everywhere, hiding from Him is impossible. This must be talking about His manifest presence. Adam and Eve were hiding from being "made known." Later, in Exodus 33:14–15, God tells Moses His presence will go with the Israelites. This also cannot refer to His omnipresence. God is speaking here of His manifest presence as He promises to walk with His people daily like He did with Adam and Eve. Manifest means to make known, seen, recognized, and understood. God wants to make His presence known to us every day.

Leaving His Presence

We cannot leave the omnipresence of God, but we can leave His manifest presence. How does this happen? We leave His presence when we don't do what He tells us to do. God told Adam and Eve not to eat from the tree; when they disobeyed, they left His presence. God told Cain to change his attitude toward his brother Abel, but Cain chose to murder his brother and left the presence of God. God told Jonah to go to Nineveh, but the prophet ran the opposite direction:

Now the word of the Lord came to Jonah the son of Amittai, saying, "Arise, go to Nineveh, that great city, and cry out against it; for their wickedness has come up before Me." But Jonah arose to flee to Tarshish *from the presence of the Lord*. He went down to Joppa, and found a ship going to Tarshish; so he paid the fare, and went down into it, to go with them to Tarshish *from the presence of the Lord* (Jonah 1:1-3, emphasis added).

What do you do when you hear God's voice? If God speaks to you and you do not obey Him, you leave His presence. I am speaking of willful disobedience, not making mistakes. In life, we can be in the same house with someone (such as a spouse) and not experience the joy of the presence of that person. In the same way, you can come to church, pray, and read the Bible every day, but if you are not living in obedience, you will not fully experience God's presence.

Entering His Presence

There are many ways to enter God's presence; in this series we will focus on worship.

Oh come, let us sing to the Lord!
Let us shout joyfully to the Rock of our salvation.
Let us come before His presence with thanksgiving;
Let us shout joyfully to Him with psalms (Psalm 95:1-2).

Make a joyful shout to the Lord, all you lands!
Serve the Lord with gladness;
Come before His presence with singing (Psalm 100:1-2).

Music, singing, and praise and worship may be more important than we think to entering the presence of the Lord. I am not talking about being musically inclined; I'm talking about praising the One who is worthy of praise. You don't have to be a musician to worship God through musical worship. Music lifts us up and moves us deep in our souls.

Sadly, some of us only enter God's presence once a week. God wants you to worship Him and enter His presence every day. Things may not always be perfect in your life, but when you spend time in His presence, the peace and joy of the Lord will be with you in both the good days and the bad.

NOTES

_____

_____

_____

_____

_____

_____

_____

_____

_____

TALK

These questions can be used for group discussion or personal reflection.

Question 1

Adam and Eve knew God in the most intimate way, yet once they sinned, they hid from Him (Genesis 3:8). We sometimes do the same thing. Why do you think this is?

_____

_____

_____

_____

Question 2

Although we can never leave the omnipresence of God, we can leave His manifest presence. Review the stories of Cain (Genesis 4:16) and Jonah (Jonah 1:3). Did they react in willful disobedience, or did they simply make mistakes? What is the difference?

_____

_____

_____

_____

Question 3

There are times when we willfully disobey God. How do our choices affect our ability to sense His presence?

_____

_____

_____

_____

Question 4

Because of God's mercy, He forgives us when we ask. What are some ways we can open the door to God's presence?

_____

_____

_____

_____

Question 5

Can someone attend a church service but still miss out on God's presence? Why or why not?

_____

_____

_____

_____

PRAY

If studying alone, ask the Holy Spirit to reveal the truth about Himself to you. If in a group, take some time to pray for each other as you think about the truths discussed in this session.

EXPLORE

Do you want to go deeper with this teaching? Here are some additional things to think about, pray for, or write about in your journal throughout the next week.

Key Thought

*When God tells you to do something and you don't do it, you begin leaving His presence. God wants us to **live** in His presence.*

What is the difference between *being* in God's presence and *living* in His presence?

_____

_____

_____

_____

Key Verses

Genesis 3:8; Exodus 33:14-15; Jonah 1:1-3; Psalm 95:1-2

What truths stand out to you as you read these verses?

What is the Holy Spirit saying to you through these Scriptures?

Key Question

In this introductory session, we learned God wants us to *live* in His presence. Take a few minutes to reflect. Are you entering God's presence only once a week? Are there things God has asked you to do that remain undone? How can you begin walking in obedience to His voice today?

Key Prayer

Lord, I want to live in Your presence. Forgive me for the times I have hidden from You, whether due to simple mistakes or outright disobedience. I want to walk and talk with You every day. In Jesus' name, Amen.

2

HIS INSTRUMENTS

Music plays a major part in our culture and in our worship today. It has also played a central role in worship in heaven.

RECAP

In the previous session, we learned about the manifest presence of God in our lives. This is different from His omnipresence or inner presence. We can leave God's manifest presence through willful disobedience, and we can enter into His manifest presence with worship.

Describe any moments this week, outside the church service, when you recognized that you were in God's manifest presence.

ENGAGE

As a young child, what did you want to be when you grew up?

WATCH

Watch "His Instruments."

- Look for the original function God intended for Satan to fulfill.
- Watch for the role of the different kinds of instruments in worship.

(If you are not able to watch this teaching on video, read the following. Otherwise, skip to the **Talk** section after viewing.)

READ

As we saw in the first session, worship plays an important role in entering the manifest presence of God, both on earth and in heaven. To understand the nature of music, we need to understand the nature of musical instruments and how they are to be used in our worship to God. Interestingly, Satan plays a key role in this understanding.

Why Did Satan Fall?

Most believers know Satan is an angel who fell from heaven, and one-third of the angels fell with him. Why did he fall? I believe the one word to describe why Satan fell is *worship*.

"How you are fallen from heaven,
O Lucifer, son of the morning!
How you are cut down to the ground,
You who weakened the nations!
For you have said in your heart:
'I will ascend into heaven,
I will exalt my throne above the stars of God;
I will also sit on the mount of the congregation
On the farthest sides of the north;
I will ascend above the heights of the clouds,
I will be like the Most High.'
Yet you shall be brought down to Sheol,
To the lowest depths of the Pit" (Isaiah 14:12–15).

Satan (originally named Lucifer) was created to lead worship. This passage describes the five "I wills" he said in his heart that caused him to fall from heaven, all of which have to do with being lifted up or exalted:

1. I will *ascend* (higher—he was already in heaven).
2. I will *exalt* my throne above the stars.
3. I will *sit on the mount* of the congregation.
4. I will *ascend* above the heights of the clouds.
5. I will *be like* God Most High.

(Note that Satan emphasizes God being Most High, not holy or loving or just.)

Satan wanted to be higher than God, but God responded by sending him in the opposite direction: "down to Sheol, to the lowest depths of the pit" (v. 15).

Satan wanted to be worshipped—to be like God and have people honor him. Many people think of Adam as the first ever to have sinned, but actually Satan was the original sinner. As part of the human race, we are born with an Adamic nature, but as sinners, we are also born with a Satanic nature. Our sinful nature wants to be lifted up and exalted.

Satan wants to turn the conversation to himself, but Jesus always turned it to God the Father or God the Holy Spirit. Jesus said He didn't do or say anything unless the Father told Him or showed Him. He said the One coming after Him (the Holy Spirit) would do even greater works. The more we become like Christ, the more we will turn the conversation off ourselves and onto God and others.

Satan started out wanting to be worshipped. He wants it now, and he will want it in the future. Revelation 12:9 says that in the end times people will worship the dragon (Satan). Revelation 13:4 says they will worship the beast and ask, "Who is able to make war with him?" You may recognize this verse as a line from Old Testament songs about God. Satan's plan has been, is now, and will be to try to steal worship from God.

He even tried to get Jesus to worship him. During Jesus' time in the wilderness, Satan showed Him many things and said, "All these things I will give You if You will fall down and worship me"

(Matthew 4:9). Notice the phrase "fall down and worship." Worship is always expressed. Why? Because worship is love, and love is always expressed. Many people come to church and do not express their worship. They may say, "I'm just not an expressive person" but have no trouble being expressive during a sports game, concert, etc. When you come to church, your children need to see you expressing your love to God.

Who Created Instruments?

God did. In Isaiah 14:11, God talks to Lucifer about "your stringed instruments." Satan was created to be a worship leader.

> Moreover the word of the Lord came to me, saying, "Son of man, take up a lamentation for the king of Tyre, and say to him, 'Thus says the Lord God:
>
> *You were the seal of perfection,*
> *Full of wisdom and perfect in beauty.*
> *You were in Eden, the garden of God;*
> *Every precious stone was your covering:*
> *The sardius, topaz, and diamond,*
> *Beryl, onyx, and jasper,*
> *Sapphire, turquoise, and emerald with gold.*
> *The workmanship of your timbrels and pipes*
> *Was prepared for you on the day you were created.*
> *You were the anointed cherub who covers;*
> *I established you;*

You were on the holy mountain of God;
You walked back and forth in the midst of fiery stones.
You were perfect in your ways from the day you were created,
Till iniquity was found in you.
By the abundance of your trading
You became filled with violence within,
And you sinned;
Therefore I cast you as a profane thing
Out of the mountain of God;
And I destroyed you, O covering cherub,
From the midst of the fiery stones" (Ezekiel 28:11–16).

Ezekiel's prophecy about Satan (king of Tyre) says he was an anointed cherub (angel) who covers, which means one who had authority. He was one of three archangels, along with Michael and Gabriel. This passage says Satan was born perfect in his ways until sin caused him to be cast out.

Ezekiel says Satan was kicked out of heaven due to *trading*. This word in Hebrew means merchandising—siphoning off money from the owner of a store. That's what Satan did with worship. He was the worship leader in heaven before the fall, and worship was supposed pass through his hands to the rightful owner, God. Satan took some of the worship for himself, and for this, he was immediately kicked out of heaven. God alone is worthy to be worshipped.

Satan was the worship leader in heaven because he was created with instruments. The three archangels correlate with the three pillars on which the Church is built: the Word, prayer, and worship. Michael rules over prayer; every time you see him in Scripture, he is answering prayer, such as in Daniel 10. Gabriel rules over the Word of the Lord; he brought the message to Zechariah about his son, John the Baptist, and to Mary about her Son, Jesus.

Lucifer (Satan) *used to* rule over worship. Isaiah 14 references Satan's stringed instruments, and Ezekiel 28:13 mentions timbrels and pipes:

> "The workmanship of your timbrels and pipes was prepared for you on the day you were created."

Timbrels are tambourines (percussion instruments), and pipes are wind instruments. All three types of instruments (strings, percussion, and wind) were prepared for Satan on the day he was created. All instruments fall into these three classifications, and we also were created with all three within us: percussion (clapping and stomping), strings (vocal cords), and wind (the vocal cords working when wind passes over them).

More happens when musical instruments are played and we sing than we often realize. Musical instruments were intended to worship God (1 Chronicles 13:8) and can be used to prophesy (1 Chronicles 25:1). We are His instruments on earth. In 2 Chronicles 5:14, the house of God was filled with the glory of the Lord from the music and praise of the worshippers.

What Did God Do?

> The earth was without form, and void; and darkness *was* on the face of the deep. And the Spirit of God was hovering over the face of the waters (Genesis 1:2)

Most theologians believe this was when God threw Satan out of heaven. Satan brought chaos, emptiness, and darkness to the earth.

> Then God said, "Let there be light"; and there was light (Genesis 1:3).

The first thing God was to restore light and dispel the darkness. Then He brought form by creating a light for day (sun) and a light for night (moon). He created the stars and land and sea. God filled the emptiness with plants, mountains, trees, and all kinds of living things.

But there was one thing missing: who would sing and give glory to God now? He reached into the dirt, blew His Spirit into it, and created man. Man would now be God's worship leader, and furthermore, he would crush Satan's head (Romans 16:20).

The problem occurred when Satan came to God's new worship leaders (Adam and Eve) and told them the exact same thing that caused him to fall—they could be like God. They bought into the temptation, and chaos, emptiness, and darkness came back into the world.

Two thousand years ago, God said again, "Let there be light." He sent His Son, Jesus, the Light of the world. God created you in His image. He created you with instruments to worship and praise Him. When you use your instruments, the glory of the Lord will fill your house, the Church, and the world. Instruments are so much more important than you think.

NOTES

_____

_____

_____

_____

_____

_____

_____

_____

_____

_____

_____

_____

TALK

These questions can be used for group discussion or personal reflection.

Question 1

Worship is love, and true love is always expressed. Why do you think some of us have trouble expressing love?

_____

_____

_____

_____

Question 2

Examine Isaiah 14:13–15. What are Satan's five "I will" statements? What was God's response to this rebellious attitude?

_____

_____

_____

_____

Question 3
Read Matthew 4:8-10. When the devil encountered Jesus in the wilderness, what did he want Jesus to do? What did Jesus say to rebuke him?

_____

_____

_____

Question 4
The words in Isaiah 14:11 and Ezekiel 28:13 were spoken to kings but aptly describe Satan. What are the characteristics that pertain to him in these verses?

_____

_____

_____

Question 5
Satan wanted to be like God. In the Garden of Eden, he told Adam and Eve they could be like God. This desire led to rebellion. How did God redeem us from this sin?

_____

_____

_____

_____

PRAY

If studying alone, ask the Holy Spirit to reveal the truth about Himself to you. If in a group, take some time to pray for each other as you think about the truths discussed in this session.

EXPLORE

Do you want to go deeper with this teaching? Here are some additional things to think about, pray for, or write about in your journal throughout the next week.

Key Thought

God created you in His image. And He created you with instruments to worship and to praise the Lord. When you worship Him, and you use your instruments, the glory of the Lord will fill this house.

In what form did God appear when He filled the house with His presence (2 Chronicles 5:13-14)? What moves God to fill our houses with His presence?

_____

_____

_____

_____

Key Verses
Isaiah 14:12-15; Ezekiel 28:11-16; 1 Chronicles 13:8; Matthew 4:8-9
What truths stand out to you as you read these verses?

_____

_____

_____

What is the Holy Spirit saying to you through these Scriptures?

_____

_____

_____

_____

Key Question
Given that we were created by God with instruments to worship Him, how can I ensure I will use these instruments to His greatest glory?

Key Prayer
Father, I want to be Your instrument. I will give my praise and worship to You because I love You. You are the King of kings and Lord of lords! May Your glory fill my house. In Jesus' name, Amen.

3

HIS DESIRE

God designed you to be in a relationship with Him. He loves you, and His desire is for you to love Him in return.

RECAP

In the previous session, we learned how God created us with instruments to worship Him. Satan was the original heavenly worship leader, but he fell from grace due to his desire to steal worship from God.

Have you been able to identify the gifts—the instruments—God has given you to worship Him?

> ENGAGE
>
> Did you have a favorite song in elementary school? Can you still remember the lyrics?
>
> WATCH
>
> Watch "His Desire."
> - Consider how God created you from Himself.
> - Watch for how we are like God and how we can love Him.
>
> (If you are not able to watch this teaching on video, read the following. Otherwise, skip to the **Talk** section after viewing.)

READ

Does God, who is completely self-sufficient, self-existent, and self-sustaining, have a desire? And if He does, what is it?

God Made Me *from* Him

In the beginning, God created some things, and He made some things. The things He created were formed out of nothing. For example, God said, "Let there be light," and there was light. The things God made, on the other hand, were formed out of something else. When God wanted to make something, He spoke to what He wanted it to be made out of, to be sustained by, and to be returned to.

When God made trees, He spoke to the earth (dirt); He wanted trees to come from dirt, be sustained by dirt, and return to dirt. In Genesis 1:20, fish were brought forth and sustained through water.

In Genesis 1:24, the earth brought forth living creatures—animals that would come from, be sustained by, and go back to earth.

When God wanted us, He spoke to Himself. He wanted us to come from Him, be sustained by Him, and return to Him. He *made* us in His image (Genesis 1:26). Now, some may ask about God forming us out of the dust of the earth. It is true that our bodies came from dirt, are sustained by dirt, and will one day return to dirt. However, our *spirits* come from God, are sustained by God, and will go back to God.

What would happen if a plant said to the dirt, "I'm pulling out. I'm going to make it on my own"? It would die. Man said to God, "I'm pulling out. I'm going to make it on my own." God said man would die the day he did. When Adam and Eve sinned, their bodies did not die immediately, but their spirits did (Ephesians 2:1 and John 10:10).

God Made Me **like** Him

If God made me in His image, and He has a desire, then what is His desire?

God made someone just like Him, a replica of Himself—Adam. Adam had no impure thoughts or wants, but he did have a desire. Genesis 2:20 says,

> So Adam gave names to all cattle, to the birds of the air, and to every beast of the field. But for Adam there was not found a helper comparable to him.

Adam was looking for something because he had a desire he couldn't express: a companion. God met this desire by causing Adam to go to sleep, removing one of his ribs, and making a woman out of it. When Adam woke up, he saw this new "animal" and named her *Woman* ("from man").

How did God know the only thing that would satisfy the desire of Adam's heart was a bride? Because God has the same desire. God created you in His image, which means He created you with a will. Love is a choice. You want someone to *choose* to love you, not to have to love you. It is not love if you force it.

God Made Me to **Love** Him

One of the primary expressions of love is worship. God's greatest desire is you—that you would choose to love Him. One theme appears over and over again in Scripture: God's desire for Him to be our God and for us to be His people.

- Exodus 6:7
- Leviticus 26:12
- Jeremiah 7:23; 11:4; 24:7; 30:22; 31:33
- Ezekiel 11:20; 14:11; 36:28; 37:23, 27
- Hosea 2:23
- Zechariah 8:8; 13:9
- 2 Corinthians 6:16
- Hebrews 8:10
- Revelation 21:1-3

God wants us to be His people. We are His desire. But because of sin, somebody had to die. Jesus Himself made the choice to die—to be the ultimate sacrifice—so that His bride might live.

NOTES

_____

_____

_____

_____

_____

_____

_____

_____

_____

_____

_____

_____

_____

_____

_____

_____

TALK

These questions can be used for group discussion or personal reflection.

Question 1

Read Genesis 2:20-22. What is the difference between the things God created and the things God made?

_____

_____

_____

_____

Question 2

When God wanted something, He spoke to what He wanted it to be made out of, to be sustained by, and to be returned to. How does this process relate to our bodies and spirits?

_____

_____

_____

_____

Question 3

What was Adam's desire? How did God know this?

_____

_____

_____

_____

Question 4

If God is all-powerful, why does He not simply force us to love Him?

_____

_____

_____

_____

Question 5

What is the common theme of the following passages: Exodus 6:7; Leviticus 26:12; Jeremiah 7:23; 2 Corinthians 6:16; Revelation 21:1–3?

_____

_____

_____

_____

PRAY

If studying alone, ask the Holy Spirit to reveal the truth about Himself to you. If in a group, take some time to pray for each other as you think about the truths discussed in this session.

EXPLORE

Do you want to go deeper with this teaching? Here are some additional things to think about, pray for, or write about in your journal throughout the next week.

Key Thought

How did God know that the only thing that would satisfy the desire of Adam's heart was a bride? How did God know that? Because God has the same desire.

We are God's desire. This is why He made us and sustained us and why we will return to Him. He made us to be His bride. Quietly reflect on what this means.

_____

_____

_____

_____

Key Verses
Genesis 1:11, 20, 24, 26; 2:20; Ezekiel 11:20; 14:11
What truths stand out to you as you read these verses?

_____

_____

_____

What is the Holy Spirit saying to you through these Scriptures?

_____

_____

_____

Key Question
Have you ever thought about what it means for the Church to be Jesus' bride? How do you picture the wedding feast between Jesus and His bride in the book of Revelation?

Key Prayer
Father, I love You. I desire to spend time with You and know You in a deeper way. I am sorry for the times I have strayed to follow my own way. I want to follow Your way. In Jesus' name, Amen.

4

HIS ENTRYWAY

King Solomon asked for wisdom to know how to "go out and come in." Leaders need to know how to lead people in and lead people out. There are entryways to God's presence.

RECAP

In the previous session, we learned that God's desire is for us to be His bride. He loves us, and He wants us to love Him in return.

Did you experience the love of God any differently this week?

ENGAGE

If you could meet anyone from the Bible, who would it be?

WATCH

Watch "His Entryway."

- Look for the reasons biblical leaders lead people out and in.
- Consider the personal battles in your life and how you may enter God's presence.

(If you are not able to watch this teaching on video, read the following. Otherwise, skip to the **Talk** section after viewing.)

READ

Many people know that Solomon asked God for wisdom, but few actually know why. In 1 Kings 3:7, the new king prays:

> "Now, O Lord my God, You have made Your servant king instead of my father David, but I *am* a little child; I do not know *how* to go out or come in."

His father, David, knew how to go out and come in, but Solomon did not. What did this mean? And why was this so important?

The phrase "go out and come in" appears multiple times in the Old Testament, such as when Moses prays about finding a successor in Numbers 27:16–17:

"Let the Lord, the God of the spirits of all flesh, set a man over the congregation, who may **go out** before them and **go in** before them, who may **lead them out** and **bring them in**, that the congregation of the Lord may not be like sheep which have no shepherd" (emphasis added).

Then, when Moses announces Joshua as his successor, he begins by saying, "I *am* one hundred and twenty years old today. I can no longer go out and come in" (Deuteronomy 31:2). Several chapters earlier, in Deuteronomy 28:6, God promises those who obey His voice will be blessed coming in and going out.

Even Jesus uses this same phrase in the New Testament:

"I am the gate; whoever enters through me will be saved. He will come in and go out, and find pasture" (John 10:9 NIV).

What does this phrase "going out and coming in" mean? We find the definition in Joshua 14:11, when Caleb declares:

"As yet I *am as* strong this day as on the day that Moses sent me; just as my strength *was* then, so now *is* my strength for war, both for going out and for coming in."

Going out and coming in were military terms. Solomon knew his father was a warrior; David knew how to lead the people out and bring them in. Solomon did not know how to go to war or how to come back from it.

> Now Saul was afraid of David, because the Lord was with him,
> but had departed from Saul. Therefore Saul removed him from his
> presence, and made him his captain over a thousand; and he went
> out and came in before the people. And David behaved wisely in
> all his ways, and the Lord *was* with him. Therefore, when Saul saw
> that he behaved very wisely, he was afraid of him. But all Israel and
> Judah loved David, because he went out and came in before them
> (1 Samuel 18:12-16).

Israel loved David because he went out and came in before them. What did these leaders come in to do? They came in to worship. Regardless of whether the war was over, won, or lost, they came back in to worship in the house of God.

If the war was lost, they came in and repented.

If the war was won, they came in and rejoiced.

If the war was still going on, they came in to get refreshed and go back out.

The same is true for our spiritual lives today. When we come to church after losing a battle, we repent. When we come to church after having won a battle, we rejoice. And when we come to church and are in middle of a struggle, we get refreshed.

Worship Brings God's Presence in Our Lives

In 1 Samuel 18:12, Saul was afraid because the Lord was with David. David was a great king because God was with him. He had learned how to live in the presence of God long before he became king. He was a true worshipper who wrote and sang songs to God.

When we go out, we don't go out *from* the presence of God—we go out *with* the presence of God. If you don't come into the presence of God, you have nothing to go out with. Worship brings His presence into our lives.

Worship Brings God's Fear in Our Lives

In 1 Samuel 18:15, Scripture again says Saul was afraid of David. God had left Saul, and an evil spirit had come upon him. Because God was with David, the evil spirit was afraid of David and of God's presence on him.

Think about walking around each day with the presence of God close by. Is a demon going to attack you when God is right there? No. God's presence brings the fear of the Lord on our enemy.

Worship Brings God's Wisdom in Our Lives

First Samuel 18:14 says, "David behaved wisely in all his ways, and the Lord *was* with him." It was David's wisdom that Saul expressed fear of in verse 15.

Solomon was wise because he asked God to teach him what his father knew. Yes, David was a warrior who knew how to come out. But David was also a worshipper who knew how to come in. Solomon learned how to come into the presence of God.

David behaved wisely because the Lord was with him. When we live in His presence, He is right there to answer our questions and guide us. If we want to know how to respond when things become difficult, we respond with the wisdom of God because He is right there. We can go to a whole new level of living in the presence of God when it is something we do every day.

> Now when the queen of Sheba heard of the fame of Solomon, she came to Jerusalem to test Solomon with hard questions, *having* a very great retinue, camels that bore spices, gold in abundance, and precious stones; and when she came to Solomon, she spoke with him about all that was in her heart. So Solomon answered all her questions; there was nothing so difficult for Solomon that he could not explain it to her. And when the queen of Sheba had seen the wisdom of Solomon, the house that he had built, the food on his table, the seating of his servants, the service of his waiters and their apparel, his cupbearers and their apparel, and his entryway by which he went up to the house of the LORD, there was no more spirit in her (2 Chronicles 9:1-4).

The Queen of Sheba was reported to be the wisest and wealthiest person alive—until Solomon. She came to prove herself superior by testing Solomon's wisdom with riddles and proverbs. She also wanted to see his wealth, and she brought with her 9,000 pounds of gold (approximately $166 million in today's currency).

Solomon answered all her questions. There was nothing he could not explain. When the queen saw Solomon's wisdom, the way his house was managed (the good food, the order, and the excellence), and his entryway into the presence of God—she had no argument or breath to speak against him.

In Ezekiel 46:9, God says:

"But when the people of the land come before the Lord on the appointed feast days, whoever enters by way of the north gate to worship shall go out by way of the south gate; and whoever enters by way of the south gate shall go out by way of the north gate. He shall not return by way of the gate through which he came, but shall go out through the opposite gate."

Why would God say this? Why would He tell His people to use a different door than the one they used to enter worship? Remember, everything in the Old Testament is an example to us. God says that every time we come into His presence, we will leave differently from the way we came in. If you come in sad, you will leave glad. If you come in hurting, you will leave healed. If you come in tired, you will leave refreshed. When you come in to worship, you will leave changed.

NOTES

_____

_____

_____

_____

TALK

These questions can be used for group discussion or personal reflection.

Question 1

Read 1 Kings 3:7, Numbers 27:16–17, and Joshua 14:11. According to these Scriptures, what must a leader know how to do?

_____

_____

_____

_____

Question 2

Why was Saul afraid of David (1 Samuel 18:12, 15)? How do these verses apply to the spiritual battles we face today?

_____

_____

_____

_____

Question 3
How can we enter the presence of God like King David did?

_____

_____

_____

_____

Question 4
Read 2 Chronicles 9:4. What did the Queen of Sheba notice about King Solomon's household? What was her reaction?

_____

_____

_____

_____

Question 5
In Ezekiel 46:9, God tells the people of Israel to enter His house by one door and to leave by a different one. What can we learn from this instruction? Does entering God's presence change us, and if so, in what way?

_____

_____

_____

_____

PRAY

If studying alone, ask the Holy Spirit to reveal the truth about Himself to you. If in a group, take some time to pray for each other as you think about the truths discussed in this session.

EXPLORE

Do you want to go deeper with this teaching? Here are some additional things to think about, pray for, or write about in your journal throughout the next week.

Key Thought

*When we go out, we don't go out **from** the presence of God—we go out **with** the presence of God. If you don't come into the presence of God, you have nothing to go out with. Worship brings His presence into our lives.*

Why is it so important for believers to go out with the presence of God?

_____

_____

_____

_____

Key Verses

1 Kings 3:5-7; 1 Samuel 18:12-16; 2 Chronicles 9:1-4; Ezekiel 46:9
   What truths stand out to you as you read these verses?

_____

_____

_____

What is the Holy Spirit saying to you through these Scriptures?

_____

_____

_____

Key Question

How do you view the act of worship? Is it something you only do at church on Sundays? Or is it an entryway into God's presence, where you find strength and help for all your battles?

Key Prayer

Lord, we worship You as our heavenly Father, Almighty God, and the King of kings. We thank You that when we come to You in worship, Your presence stays with us. We have no need to fear any person or adversary. In Jesus' name, Amen.

5

HIS PLAN

Sin pulls us away from God's presence. The idols we create in our hearts can cause presumption, estrangement, and spiritual deafness—all of which have serious consequences for our lives as believers. God has a plan, though, and He will help us overcome the strongholds of sin.

RECAP

In the previous session, we learned that we enter into God's presence through worship, and His presence goes out with us to help us fight our battles.

Did you worship more often this week? Did it feel different knowing that you had more of the presence of God when you came out than when you went in?

ENGAGE

Do you have an idea for an invention? If so, what would it be? What problem would it solve or improve?

WATCH

Watch "His Plan."

- Look at how sin can manifest itself as idolatry in our lives.
- Consider what some of the consequences of your thoughts might be.

(If you are not able to watch this teaching on video, read the following. Otherwise, skip to the **Talk** section after viewing.)

READ

God wants us to live in His presence all the time, but sin pulls us away from constant communion with Him. After Adam and Eve sinned, they hid themselves from God's presence (Genesis 3:8). Willful sin (not just mistakes) pulls us away from God. The following passage from Ezekiel shows how Satan takes sin and uses it to form strongholds over us. When we serve these strongholds, we leave God's presence.

> Now some of the elders of Israel came to me and sat before me. And the word of the Lord came to me, saying, "Son of man, these men have set up their idols in their hearts, and put before them that which causes them to stumble into iniquity. Should I let Myself be inquired of at all by them?

Therefore speak to them, and say to them, 'Thus says the Lord God: *Everyone of the house of Israel who sets up his idols in his heart, and puts before him what causes him to stumble into iniquity, and then comes to the prophet, I the Lord will answer him who comes, according to the multitude of his idols, that I may seize the house of Israel by their heart, because they are all estranged from Me by their idols.*'

Therefore say to the house of Israel, 'Thus says the Lord God: *Repent, turn away from your idols, and turn your faces away from all your abominations. For anyone of the house of Israel, or of the strangers who dwell in Israel, who separates himself from Me and sets up his idols in his heart and puts before him what causes him to stumble into iniquity, then comes to a prophet to inquire of him concerning Me, I the Lord will answer him by Myself. I will set My face against that man and make him a sign and a proverb, and I will cut him off from the midst of My people. Then you shall know that I am the Lord.*

And if the prophet is induced to speak anything, I the Lord have induced that prophet, and I will stretch out My hand against him and destroy him from among My people Israel. And they shall bear their iniquity; the punishment of the prophet shall be the same as the punishment of the one who inquired, that the house of Israel may no longer stray from Me, nor be profaned anymore with all their transgressions, but that they may be My people and I may be their God, says the Lord God" (Ezekiel 14:1–11).

God has always been concerned about the heart. What is an idol, though? The word *idol* means "image," as seen in the second commandment (Exodus 20:4). If an idol is an image, then idolatry is worshipping that image. Image is the root of the word *imagina-tion*. If you think about (or imagine) something more than you think about God, it is very possible you have an idol in your heart. Here are three ways to determine if this is true for you:

Presumption

In Ezekiel 14:3, men put before them what caused them to sin. If you have an idol, you will cater to it and make plans to sin. Romans 13:14 says to make no provision for the flesh, but that is exactly what we often do. We start thinking and planning. We make up a story and begin to cover up the truth. We say to ourselves that we can always "repent" and ask for forgiveness later. However, this attitude is presuming on the grace of God.

Jeroboam did just that. He built altars in Dan in the north and Bethel in the south. He built a replica of Solomon's temple and told the people that if traveling to Jerusalem to worship was too much trouble, they could use these alternatives. Jeroboam also built idols for other gods. He made golden calves and said, "Here are your gods ... which brought you up from the land of Egypt" (1 Kings 12:28). The people could worship the god of mammon and the God of Israel; however, Jesus clearly teaches in Matthew 6:24, "You cannot serve God and mammon."

You must choose to do what God says *or* what you think is best. You cannot live in God's presence if you have an idol in your heart.

Estrangement

Ezekiel 14:5 says the people of Israel were estranged from God because of their idols. In Hebrew *estrangement* refers to a married woman who lives with another man in an adulterous relationship. As believers Jesus is our husband, and we are married to God. Having idols in our heart is having an affair against God.

The prophet Jeremiah says Israel "played the harlot," and "she defiled the land and committed adultery with stones and trees" (Jeremiah 3:6, 9). Stones and trees were used for making altars and sacrifices. The Israelites committed spiritual adultery by building altars and making sacrifices to other gods.

In Jeremiah 3:14, God says, "'Return, O backsliding children,' says the Lord; 'for I am married to you.'" Sin will not affect God's love for you, but it will affect your love for Him.

Spiritual Deafness

In Ezekiel 14, the elders of Israel went to the prophet because they themselves could not hear what God was saying. Isaiah 59:2 says,

> Your iniquities have separated you from your God;
> And your sins have hidden *His* face from you,
> So that He will not hear.

Nor will He speak. We can live in constant communion with the Holy Spirit, but when we have sin in our lives and idols in our hearts, we turn down the Holy Spirit's voice and turn up the idols'. We see this pattern of listening to idols throughout Scripture. The number one thing that prevents people from hearing God is sin. Worse yet, you will begin to think the voice you do hear is God. But it's not. It's the demonic spirit behind the idol.

Consequences

Ezekiel 14:10 says the prophet will bear the iniquity of the people and have their same punishment. In this verse, the same word is translated *punishment* and *iniquity*. If someone in sin consults a prophet, who in turn does nothing about the sin, then this prophet has the same idol in his heart.

Iniquity (punishment) literally means the consequences of sin, which can be passed on to the third and fourth generation. All sin has consequences. The ultimate wage of sin is death, and God does not want to see His people suffer.

Failure to take a stand against sin makes us hypocrites. In ancient Greece, an actor was called a *hypocrite*, which came from the Greek words "speak underneath." All actors wore masks and spoke out, pretending to be the person under the mask. God does not want us to act like this.

There are three steps to idolatry. First, we feel something is inconvenient (like having a quiet time or going to church). Second, we find something else that is more convenient. Third, we begin including other things (like other gods).

I hope Ezekiel 14 convicts you, as it did me, about the evil of idols. Conviction can bring great joy and victory. Even if you're feeling convicted, you are not a bad person. Remember that you are in a war, but you are also a child of God. In spite of Satan's efforts, Ezekiel 14:5 says God can seize His people by the heart. The only reason God speaks to us about the idols in our hearts is to bring us back to Himself. His plan for us is good!

NOTES

_____

_____

_____

_____

_____

_____

_____

_____

_____

_____

_____

_____

TALK

These questions can be used for group discussion or personal reflection.

Question 1

How does Satan use a person's imagination to set up an idol inside his or her heart? How does idolatry interfere with our relationship with God?

_____

_____

_____

_____

Question 2

How do our thoughts and actions change when we begin making "provision for the flesh" (Romans 13:14)?

_____

_____

_____

_____

Question 3
According to Ezekiel 14:5, what is God's response when we break
the second commandment (found in Exodus 20:4)?

_____

_____

_____

_____

Question 4
Read Isaiah 59:2. What happens to our communication with God
when we allow strongholds to form in our hearts?

_____

_____

_____

_____

Question 5
Does having an idol in your heart make you a bad person? What
should you do if you feel convicted in this area?

_____

_____

_____

_____

PRAY

If studying alone, ask the Holy Spirit to reveal the truth about Himself to you. If in a group, take some time to pray for each other as you think about the truths discussed in this session.

EXPLORE

Do you want to go deeper with this teaching? Here are some additional things to think about, pray for, or write about in your journal throughout the next week.

Key Thought

Sin is spiritual adultery. Sin is leaving God, going and committing adultery, and then coming back and slipping in bed with God as if nothing happened. That's what sin is. And that's what an idol will do. It will cause you to be estranged from God.

How do strongholds affect God's love for us and our love for Him?

_____

_____

_____

_____

Key Verses
Ezekiel 14:1-11; Romans 13:14; Exodus 20:4; Isaiah 59:2
What truths stand out to you as you read these verses?

_____

_____

_____

What is the Holy Spirit saying to you through these Scriptures?

_____

_____

_____

Key Question
How can we as Christians guard our hearts against the stronghold of idolatry?

Key Prayer
Lord, we turn our hearts to You. Show us any idol we've allowed to separate us from You. We want no other gods before You. Help us to love and serve You with all our hearts. In Jesus' name, Amen.

6

HIS THANKSGIVING

We can live continually in God's presence by developing a life of thanksgiving. We are grateful to God as He blesses us with His miraculous provision. We express our love and gratitude in worship.

RECAP

In the previous session, we learned how sin can manifest itself in our hearts as idols. Idols estrange us from God, and idol worship can create many consequences.

Did you experience anything this week that could have become an idol or a stronghold in your heart? If so, how did you deal with it?

ENGAGE

Do you look forward to a special holiday recipe? What is it, and why is it important to you?

WATCH

Watch "His Thanksgiving."

- Look for the many expressions of thanks in Hebrew.
- Consider how your worship may proceed from the miracles you have seen or know of.

(If you are not able to watch this teaching on video, read the following. Otherwise, skip to the **Talk** section after viewing.)

READ

Americans are very familiar with the Thanksgiving holiday. The name of this special day comes from two words: "thanks" and "giving." Some people refer to praying over a meal as "giving thanks." The first biblical mention of this custom is in the Gospels; Jesus used this phrase every time He broke bread. He wanted to teach us that our daily provision is from God, and to live in His presence, we need to live a life of thanksgiving.

This account in Luke illustrates some key points about giving thanks:

Now it happened as He went to Jerusalem that He passed through the midst of Samaria and Galilee. Then as He entered a certain village, there met Him ten men who were lepers, who stood afar off.

And they lifted up *their* voices and said, "Jesus, Master, have mercy on us!"

So when He saw *them,* He said to them, "Go, show yourselves to the priests." And so it was that as they went, they were cleansed.

And one of them, when he saw that he was healed, returned, and with a loud voice glorified God, and fell down on *his* face at His feet, giving Him thanks. And he was a Samaritan.

So Jesus answered and said, "Were there not ten cleansed? But where *are* the nine? Were there not any found who returned to give glory to God except this foreigner?" And He said to him, "Arise, go your way. Your faith has made you well" (Luke 17:11-19).

Worship Is Giving Thanks

In verses 15-16, one of the healed men returns, falls on his face, and glorifies Jesus with a loud voice. Worship is all about thanking someone after you've received something. It's showing your gratitude and love. True, genuine love is always expressed. Perhaps you did not always see this in your human family, but you are in a new family now. You have a good Father, and you can express your love to Him because you have received something good from Him.

Not everyone is going to express their feelings in the same way. We all have different personalities and different ways we show our love to God. In the Old Testament, there are 11 Hebrew words for praise, with 7 dominant ones:

1. Todah: A thanksgiving choir
2. Barak: To kneel (or bow before) in thanksgiving
3. Tehillah: To sing a song of thanksgiving
4. Halal: To give thanks by being clamorously foolish (the root of our word *Hallelujah*)
5. Yadah: To give thanks with extended (or lifted) hands
6. Zamar: To give thanks with a musical instrument
7. Shabach: To give thanks in a loud tone (or shout)

These words are about expressing love and giving thanks. You'll never be a worshipper if you're not grateful. Gratitude is what causes worship to come forth. Psalm 100:4 has four of these seven words:

Enter into His gates with thanksgiving [Todah],
And into His courts with praise [Tehillah].
Be thankful [Yadah] to Him, *and* bless [Barak] His name.

Even though we have different personalities, there are Scriptural expressions of worship. Bowing, shouting, clapping, and lifting your hands are all in the Bible. But what causes gratitude? Does something precede it?

Miracles Precede Gratitude

And one of them, **when he saw that he was healed**, returned, and with a loud voice glorified God (Luke 17:15, emphasis added).

The healed man was grateful because he had received a miracle from God. You say "thank you" to someone *after* you receive something from them. This is what worship is—giving thanks. This Samaritan fell down on his face and shouted in a loud voice. Was this appropriate? I think so.

The man had been healed of leprosy, a devastating and debilitating disease. A leper could not associate with family or children but had to live in a leper colony with other lepers. As a leper, you had to warn those who came too close to you by shouting, "Unclean!" You were a social and religious outcast since many thought the disease was brought on by God's judgement. To fall down and praise Jesus in a loud voice when He healed you of leprosy would certainly be appropriate.

If you had a disease and Jesus healed you, would it be appropriate to come together and express your thanks? We were all healed of the disease of sin—and the wages of sin is death. It's okay to come together and express our love for God.

If worship comes from being grateful and gratitude comes from miracles, is there something that can cause a miracle?

Obedience Precedes Miracles

Luke 17:14 says the lepers were cleansed "as they went." Their going emphasized their obedience. They were not cleansed when Jesus spoke; they were cleansed when they obeyed. We see this pattern throughout the Bible. Moses was told to lift up his rod at the Red Sea, even though the Egyptian army was right behind him. When the Israelites came to the Jordan River at the edge of the Promised Land, God told the priests to put their feet in the water, even though the river was at flood stage. Elisha told Naaman to dip seven times in the muddy water of the Jordan river. Jesus told a man with a withered hand to "stretch out your hand" (Matthew 12:13).

At the cross, people said, "Come down off the cross that we may see and believe." But Jesus said, "Believe, and you'll see." What is God telling you to do that you're not doing, that could release a miracle in your life?

The context of the miracle of the 10 healed lepers is interesting. Look again at Luke 17. In verses 1–5, when Jesus tells the disciples to forgive someone, they are ready to do so. But to forgive the same person seven times in the same day? The disciples reply, "Increase our faith" (v. 5). But it does not take faith to forgive. It takes **obedience**. Jesus then explains in verses 6–10 that if they had just a little bit of faith, miracles would happen. You need to do what you're told. The servant doesn't get thanks because he does what his master commanded him to do (v. 9). You just need to obey! Then Jesus comes upon the 10 lepers and uses them as an example to His disciples, and to us, of what happens when you obey.

This passage reminds us to ask, "If this miracle hasn't happened yet, what do I need to do?" Because if I do what Jesus tells me to do, I'll see miracles in my life. And when I see miracles in my life, I'll have an attitude of gratitude. And when I have an attitude of gratitude, I'll give thanks to the Lord.

NOTES

_____

_____

_____

_____

_____

_____

_____

_____

_____

_____

_____

_____

_____

_____

_____

_____

_____

_____

_____

TALK

These questions can be used for group discussion or personal reflection.

Question 1

In the four Gospels, Jesus gave thanks every time He "broke bread." How does this illustrate that daily provision comes from God?

_____

_____

_____

_____

Question 2

Read Psalm 100:4. What expressions of praise are described in this verse?

_____

_____

_____

_____

Question 3

In Luke 17:10, Jesus says we should do what God commands. How much faith does obedience require?

Question 4

Every believer has experienced his or her own personal miracle—salvation! Have you witnessed or heard about any other miracles that made you want to express your love to God?

Question 5

In what ways do Christians express gratitude during worship? If God knows everything, including our thoughts, then why does worship have to be expressed?

PRAY

If studying alone, ask the Holy Spirit to reveal the truth about Himself to you. If in a group, take some time to pray for each other as you think about the truths discussed in this session.

EXPLORE

Do you want to go deeper with this teaching? Here are some additional things to think about, pray for, or write about in your journal throughout the next week.

Key Thought

[At the cross,] they said, "Come down off the cross that we may see and believe." He said, "Believe, and you'll see."

What is God telling you to do that you're not doing, that could release a miracle in your life—which would release gratitude, which would release worship?

Is there something you are praying for or expecting to happen in your life for which God may just be waiting for you to obey?

_____

_____

_____

_____

Key Verses
Luke 17:1-19; Psalm 100:4
> What truths stand out to you as you read these verses?

_____

_____

_____

> What is the Holy Spirit saying to you through these Scriptures?

_____

_____

_____

Key Question
How often is it appropriate to give thanks to God for what we've received? Do worship and obedience increase our expectation to receive more miracles as we walk with God? How so?

Key Prayer
> *Lord, You see every area of our lives. We look to You for the miracles we need. Show us where we need to be obedient to Your Word. We want to worship You in an expressive way that shows our gratitude for Your extravagant love. Thank You for providing our daily needs. In Jesus' name, Amen.*

7

HIS WORSHIP

Each of us was born to be a worshipper. Worship is more than simply exalting God. Worship is love expressed. God commands us to love Him and gives us the ability to do so.

RECAP

In the previous session, we learned about giving thanks. When we obey God, miracles happen, which lead us to worship out of gratitude.

What did you learn about faith and obedience in the past week that encouraged you? Did you step out in obedience expecting a miracle to take place?

ENGAGE

What is the most memorable gift you have given at Christmas?
What makes it memorable to you?

WATCH

Watch "His Worship."
- Look for the importance of loving God.
- Consider how you express your love to God.

(If you are not able to watch this teaching on video, read the
following. Otherwise, skip to the **Talk** section after viewing.)

READ

You were born a worshipper—it's natural for you to worship. The
question is not if you are a worshipper, but what or whom do
you worship? Worship is not just singing. You can sing and not
worship. Worship is also not just exalting God. God did not create
you to exalt Him. The angels can do that; they were doing it before
creation, are doing it now, and will do it for all eternity.

Worship is *love expressed*. If it is love but not expressed, it is not
worship. If you express something, but it is not love, it is also not
worship. You were created to give and receive love from God.

Worship Is Love

God commands us to love Him. How can He do this? Because
love is a *choice*. God gives us the ability to choose to love Him.

Deuteronomy 11:1 says, "You shall love the Lord your God."
Verse 13 then promises God's blessings, "if you earnestly obey My
commandments which I command you today, **to love the Lord
your God** and serve Him with all your heart and with all your soul"
(emphasis added).

Jesus confirms this instruction in the New Testament when
questioned about the greatest commandment:

> "You shall love the Lord your God with all your heart, with all
> your soul, and with all your mind. This is *the* first and great
> commandment" (Matthew 22:37-38).

But how do we love God? When you got saved, God gave
you the ability to love Him. He gave you a brand-new heart.
Deuteronomy 30:6 says God has given us this ability for our
benefit—"that you may live."

Have you ever seen someone and thought he or she loved God
more than you do? Why is this?

Love leaks.

The heart is full of love, but love can leak out. Marriage is meant
to be "for better or for worse," but it can be difficult when the
worse actually comes. Our relationship with God is also for better
or for worse. Satan is constantly attacking us, shooting arrows into
our hearts with judgments, offenses, and lies. You can block every
flaming arrow with the shield of faith, but if an arrow gets through,

you will have a hole in your heart which can affect your relationship with God and other people. Check to see if there are any holes in your heart.

Love grows.

When your children are first born, you don't think you could possibly love them any more than you do right then. However, as your children grow, your love for them grows as well. In the same way, as we grow in our relationship with God, our love for Him will grow. If we sense our love for God is growing cold, we need to press in to Him even more. We can always be honest with God. He is not intimidated by our problems but will help us every time we ask.

Worship Is Expressed

If it's love, but it's not expressed, it's not worship. For example, if you are in a marriage, and you never express your love, it is not a good marriage. Love has to be expressed. Another way to say this is love must be communicated. God created us to communicate with Him, just as Adam and Eve walked and talked with Him in the Garden of Eden. But then sin came in ...

> And Adam knew his wife again, and she bore a son and named him Seth, "For God has appointed another seed for me instead of Abel, whom Cain killed." And as for Seth, to him also a son was born; and he named him Enosh. Then *men* began to call on the name of the Lord (Genesis 4:25–26).

In Enosh's lifetime, people first began to worship the Lord by name. Until then, every conversation with God after the fall was not initiated by people. The person in the conversation (whether Adam, Eve, or Cain) would only answer a question: *Where are you? Who told you ...? Did you ...?* Adam and Eve were driven out of the garden, and Cain was driven out of the presence of God. Not until Adam and Eve's grandson did humans begin to call out to God.

Women tend to communicate by talking and listening, and men typically communicate by watching and doing. No matter your gender, you will communicate about whatever you are passionate about. God created you with the ability to love and the ability to communicate. Men don't have to communicate the same as women do. Just take the time to express your love and appreciation to God in every situation.

NOTES

_____

_____

_____

_____

_____

_____

_____

TALK

These questions can be used for group discussion or personal reflection.

Question 1

Think of a person who loves you. How do you know they love you? Now think of a person you love. How does this person know you love them?

_____

_____

_____

_____

Question 2

We all communicate in different ways. What are some ways a person can communicate or express their love to God?

_____

_____

_____

_____

Question 3

The greatest thing we can do is love God. When we love God, we will serve Him willingly. What are some ways you can serve God in your everyday life?

_____

_____

_____

_____

Question 4

How can our love for God be hindered? Read Ephesians 6:16 and list some examples of Satan's fiery darts that would make our hearts discouraged, bitter, or angry. How can we guard against these attacks?

_____

_____

_____

_____

PRAY

If studying alone, ask the Holy Spirit to reveal the truth about Himself to you. If in a group, take some time to pray for each other as you think about the truths discussed in this session.

EXPLORE

Do you want to go deeper with this teaching? Here are some additional things to think about, pray for, or write about in your journal throughout the next week.

Key Thought

You say, "Well, I wish I were more passionate about God." Listen to me. You do love God. Because God created you with the ability to love, and He created you with the ability to communicate.

Are you comfortable with the idea of communicating with God? Explain.

_____

_____

_____

_____

Key Verses
Deuteronomy 11:1,13; 30:6; Matthew 22:35-38; Genesis 4:25-26
What truths stand out to you as you read these verses?

_____

_____

_____

What is the Holy Spirit saying to you through these Scriptures?

_____

_____

_____

Key Question
Love grows by reaching out toward a person with words and actions. What are some new ways you can worship the Lord this week?

Key Prayer
Lord, we love You. Help us express our love to You, not only in response to Your outrageous love for us but also because You are good, holy, and sovereign. You are the great I Am. Draw us nearer to You this week as we worship, for You are worthy of our love, praise, and adoration. In Jesus' name, Amen.

8

HIS CHRISTMAS

The Magi came to see the King of the Jews, expecting great things. They brought the best resources they had to offer. We should also come into the presence of God seeking great things and bringing Him our best.

RECAP

In the previous session, we learned worship is love expressed. Because of His great love for us, we all can love God and communicate our love in different ways.

Did you learn about or try some different ways of communicating with God this week?

ENGAGE

What is your favorite Christmas tradition? Do you have a fun
tradition, or is it more sentimental?

WATCH

Watch "His Christmas."

- Look for the different types of worship expressed by the Magi
  and the significance of the gifts they brought.
- Consider your personal worship and how it fits into these
  types.

(If you are not able to watch this teaching on video, read the
following. Otherwise, skip to the **Talk** section after viewing.)

READ

When Jesus came into the world, people began to show up. They
began to worship Him; they wanted to be in His presence.

Now after Jesus was born in Bethlehem of Judea in the days of
Herod the king, behold, wise men from the East came to Jerusalem,
saying, "Where is He who has been born King of the Jews? For we
have seen His star in the East and have come to worship Him."

When Herod the king heard *this*, he was troubled, and all
Jerusalem with him. And when he had gathered all the chief priests
and scribes of the people together, he inquired of them where the
Christ was to be born.

So they said to him, "In Bethlehem of Judea, for thus it is written
by the prophet:

'But you, Bethlehem, *in* the land of Judah,
Are not the least among the rulers of Judah;
For out of you shall come a Ruler
Who will shepherd My people Israel.'"

Then Herod, when he had secretly called the wise men, determined from them what time the star appeared. And he sent them to Bethlehem and said, "Go and search carefully for the young Child, and when you have found *Him,* bring back word to me, that I may come and worship Him also."

When they heard the king, they departed; and behold, the star which they had seen in the East went before them, till it came and stood over where the young Child was. When they saw the star, they rejoiced with exceedingly great joy. And when they had come into the house, they saw the young Child with Mary His mother, and fell down and worshiped Him. And when they had opened their treasures, they presented gifts to Him: gold, frankincense, and myrrh.

Then, being divinely warned in a dream that they should not return to Herod, they departed for their own country another way (Matthew 2:1–12).

Expectant Worship

Matthew 2 records the story of the Magi coming to worship Jesus. They traveled 1,000 miles expecting something to happen when they entered the presence of the King. Then they rejoiced and fell down and worshipped Him

The Greek root of *Magi* means "magic." The Magi were probably sorcerers—magicians, astrologers, and astronomers (see Daniel 2:2). These Magi were probably believers. They may have learned of the prophecy of Jesus from Persian history. Many historians and theologians believe Balaam, who the king of Moab hired to cast a spell on Israel, was the father of the Magi. God would not let Balaam put a curse on Israel. Numbers 24:17 records the prophecy about beholding a star coming out of Jacob (Israel). This may be where the Persian Magi learned of the star.

God rescued the Jewish people from the Persians through Esther. The Persians also saw that God rescued Daniel, a Jewish man, from the lions' den, and three other Jewish men were rescued from the fiery furnace. When studying their history, the Persians kept reading about the God of the Jews rescuing His people. Daniel prophesied that the Messiah would come 483 years later. Jesus was born 453 years later, and the Magi knew that the Jews began their ministry when they were 30 years old. (Joseph and David started theirs when they were 30 years old, and Daniel probably did as well.)

The Magi didn't travel on camels; they rode on Persian horses. They traveled for about nine months and approximately 1,000 miles. The Magi first went to Jerusalem to learn about the Jewish Scriptures and then went to Bethlehem when they learned this was where the Messiah was to be born. Jesus would have been anywhere from 9 to 18 months old when the Magi arrived. He was a toddler, not a baby. The Magi came into the "house," not the stable, and saw the "young Child," not a baby.

The prophecy had been passed down for hundreds of years about this Messiah, and these Persian men traveled 1,000 miles to enter His presence and worship Him. If they made that much effort to get into His presence, why don't you make just a little effort?

They were expectant. They were excited. You should have an excitement building up on Thursday and Friday, anticipating that you will be entering God's presence with His people. Of course, you should want to enter His presence every day. But there is something special about entering His presence with His people.

Expressive Worship

Matthew 2:10-11 say the Magi "rejoiced with exceedingly great joy" and "fell down and worshipped." In this passage, the second phrase means to fall down violently and be shattered—like a building collapsing in an earthquake or being imploded by dynamite.

The Magi walked into a house, saw a toddler, and were shattered in His presence. These were not unintelligent or socially unacceptable men. These were the wealthy intelligentsia of the day. They collapsed. It wouldn't be a bad idea if every now and then you collapsed in His presence.

You need to let yourself go sometimes in worship. One day, every billionaire, every atheist, and every college professor are going to fall down in His presence.

The Bible has many examples of expressive worship.

Oh, clap your hands, all you peoples!
Shout to God with the voice of triumph! (Psalm 47:1).

Oh come, let us sing to the Lord!
Let us shout joyfully to the Rock of our salvation (Psalm 95:1).

Oh come, let us worship and bow down;
Let us kneel before the Lord our Maker (Psalm 95:6).

Lift up your hands *in* the sanctuary,
And bless the Lord (Psalm 134:2).

Extravagant Worship

And when they had come into the house, they saw the young Child
with Mary His mother, and fell down and worshiped Him. And
when they had opened their treasures, they presented gifts to Him:
gold, frankincense, and myrrh (Matthew 2:11).

The three gifts of the Magi had prophetic significance:

- Gold represented royalty.
- Frankincense represented divinity (Incense: offering your
  prayers up to God).
- Myrrh represented humanity. (It was what you anointed a
  dead body with.)

These were the *three best resources* Persia offered. Do you
bring your best when you come to worship? We can be distracted

and go through the motions of worship or our quiet time and not bring our best.

Verse 11 says they opened their treasures. When people traveled at that time, they always brought more funds than they needed (usually double) to allow for unforeseen circumstances. The Magi had 36 months of resources for their 18-month round trip—their treasury. They opened it up and gave it all to the child King. They gave their offering, and they gave sacrificially. You can never separate worship and giving.

Finally, the Magi came first to Jerusalem and asked, "Where is He?" After they visited Jesus, they were divinely warned in a dream how to return home. Before they worshipped—before they entered Jesus' presence—they had to go to other people to find out what the Bible said. But after the Magi entered His presence, God spoke to them directly.

When you're not a worshipper, you will always have to ask somebody, "What does this mean?" when referring to the Bible. When you are in the habit of entering God's presence on a daily basis, God will speak directly to you.

NOTES

_____

_____

_____

_____

TALK

These questions can be used for group discussion or personal reflection.

Question 1

Does your heart stir with excitement toward the end of the week as you prepare to come to the Lord's sanctuary and worship with His people? How has this teaching influenced your view on corporate worship?

_____

_____

_____

_____

Question 2

Think of someone you really love. Can you remember an occasion when you gave an extravagant gift to this person as if you just couldn't help yourself? Why do you think giving goes with adoration?

_____

_____

_____

_____

Question 3

Gold, frankincense, and myrrh were the best resources Persia had to offer. The Magi brought their *best* gifts to Jesus. What does it mean to you to bring your best to God in worship?

_____

_____

_____

_____

Question 4

Read Matthew 2:12. Before they met Jesus, the Magi had to inquire about the Word of God from others. But once they had been in the presence of God, they heard directly from Him. How would you encourage someone to deepen their relationship with God through worship?

_____

_____

_____

_____

PRAY

If studying alone, ask the Holy Spirit to reveal the truth about Himself to you. If in a group, take some time to pray for each other as you think about the truths discussed in this session.

EXPLORE

Do you want to go deeper with this teaching? Here are some additional things to think about, pray for, or write about in your journal throughout the next week.

Key Thought

> These men walked into a house and saw a toddler and fell down violently. And they were shattered in His presence. These were the wealthy intelligentsia of the day. They collapsed. It wouldn't be a bad idea if every now and then you collapsed in His presence and were shattered.

Read Matthew 2:11. What do you think you would do if you saw Jesus here right now? Would you fall down before Him? How do you think you'll react when you see Him in heaven?

_____

_____

_____

_____

Key Verses
Matthew 2:1-12; Numbers 24:17; Psalm 47:1; 95:1, 6; 134:2
What truths stand out to you as you read these verses?

_____

_____

_____

What is the Holy Spirit saying to you through these Scriptures?

_____

_____

_____

Key Question
Will you anticipate the presence of the Lord and offer expectant, expressive, and extravagant worship to Him throughout the week?

Key Prayer
Lord, You are worthy of our praise and worship. Thank You for sending Your Son, Emmanuel, to bring us salvation, forgiveness, and healing. Thank You for inviting us into Your kingdom. We love You and adore You. In Jesus' name, Amen.

LEADER'S GUIDE

The *Living in His Presence* Leader's Guide is designed to help you lead your small group or class through the *Living in His Presence* curriculum. Use this guide along with the curriculum for a life-changing, interactive experience.

BEFORE YOU MEET

- Ask God to prepare the hearts and minds of the people in your group. Ask Him to show you how to encourage each person to integrate the principles all of you discover into your daily lives through group discussion and writing in your journals.
- Preview the video segment for the week.
- Plan how much time you'll give to each portion of your meeting (see the suggested schedule below). In case you're unable to get through all of the activities in the time you have planned, here is a list of the most important questions (from the **Talk** section) for each week.

SUGGESTED SMALL GROUP SCHEDULE

1. **Engage** and **Recap** (5 Minutes)
2. **Watch** or **Read** (20 Minutes)
3. **Talk** (25 Minutes)
4. **Pray** (10 minutes)

SESSION ONE

Q: Adam and Eve knew God in the most intimate way, yet once they sinned, they hid from Him (Genesis 3:8). We sometimes do the same thing. Why do you think this is?

Q: Because of God's mercy, He forgives us when we ask. What are some ways we can open the door to God's presence?

SESSION TWO

Q: Worship is love, and true love is always expressed. Why do you think some of us have trouble expressing love?

Q: Satan wanted to be like God. In the Garden of Eden, he told Adam and Eve they could be like God. This desire led to rebellion. How did God redeem us from this sin?

SESSION THREE

Q: Read Genesis 2:20–22. What is the difference between the things God created and the things God made?

Q: When God wanted something, He spoke to what He wanted it to be made out of, to be sustained by, and to be returned to. How does this process relate to our bodies and spirits?

SESSION FOUR

Q: How can we enter the presence of God like King David did?

Q: Why was Saul afraid of David (1 Samuel 18:12, 15)? How do these verses apply to the spiritual battles we face today?

SESSION FIVE

Q: How does Satan use a person's imagination to set up an idol inside his or her heart? How does idolatry interfere with our relationship with God?

Q: According to Ezekiel 14:5, what is God's response when we break the second commandment (found in Exodus 20:4)?

SESSION SIX

Q: Read Psalm 100:4. What expressions of praise are described in this verse?

Q: In Luke 17:10, Jesus says we should do what God commands. How much faith does obedience require?

SESSION SEVEN

Q: Think of a person who loves you. How do you know they love you? Now think of a person you love. How does this person know you love them?

Q: We all communicate in different ways. What are some ways a person can communicate or express their love to God?

SESSION EIGHT

Q: Gold, frankincense, and myrrh were the best resources Persia had to offer. The Magi brought their *best* gifts to Jesus. What does it mean to you to bring your best to God in worship?

Q: Read Matthew 2:12. Before they met Jesus, the Magi had to inquire about the Word of God from others. But once they had been in the presence of God, they heard directly from Him. How would you encourage someone to deepen their relationship with God through worship?

Remember, the goal is not necessarily to get through all of the questions. The highest priority is for the group to learn and engage in a dynamic discussion.

HOW TO USE THE CURRICULUM

This study has a simple design.

The One Thing

This is a single statement under each session title that sums up the main point—the key idea—of the session.

Recap

Recap the previous session, inviting members to share about any opportunities they have encountered throughout the week that apply to what they learned (this doesn't apply to the first week).

Engage

Ask the icebreaker question to help get people talking and feeling comfortable with one another.

Watch

Watch the videos (recommended).

Read

If you're unable to watch the videos, read these sections.

Talk

Discuss the questions.

Pray

Pray together.

Explore

Encourage members to complete the written portion in their books before the next meeting.

KEY TIPS FOR THE LEADER

- Generate participation and discussion.
- Resist the urge to teach. The goal is for great conversation that leads to discovery.
- Ask open-ended questions—questions that can't be answered with "yes" or "no" (e.g., "What do you think about that?" rather than "Do you agree?")
- When a question arises, ask the group for their input first, instead of immediately answering it yourself.
- Be comfortable with silence. If you ask a question and no one responds, rephrase the question and wait for a response. Your primary role is to create an environment where people feel comfortable to be themselves and participate, not to provide the answers to all of their questions.
- Ask the group to pray for each other from week to week, especially about key issues that arise during your group time. This is how you begin to build authentic community and encourage spiritual growth within the group.

KEYS TO A DYNAMIC SMALL GROUP

Relationships
Meaningful, encouraging relationships are the foundation of a dynamic small group. Teaching, discussion, worship, and prayer are important elements of a group meeting, but the depth of each

element is often dependent upon the depth of the relationships among members.

Availability

Building a sense of community within your group requires members to prioritize their relationships with one another. This means being available to listen, care for one another, and meet each other's needs.

Mutual Respect

Mutual respect is shown when members value each other's opinions (even when they disagree) and are careful never to put down or embarrass others in the group (including their spouses, who may or may not be present).

Openness

A healthy small group environment encourages sincerity and transparency. Members treat each other with grace in areas of weakness, allowing each other room to grow.

Confidentiality

To develop authenticity and a sense of safety within the group, each member must be able to trust that things discussed within the group will not be shared outside the group.

Shared Responsibility

Group members will share the responsibility of group meetings by using their God-given abilities to serve at each gathering. Some may greet, some may host, some may teach, etc. Ideally, each person should be available to care for others as needed.

Sensitivity

Dynamic small groups are born when the leader consistently seeks and is responsive to the guidance of the Holy Spirit, following His leading throughout the meeting as opposed to sticking to the "agenda." This guidance is especially important during the discussion and ministry time.

Fun!

Dynamic small groups take the time to have fun! Create an atmosphere for fun and be willing to laugh at yourself every now and then!

ABOUT THE AUTHOR

Robert Morris is the founding senior pastor of Gateway Church, a multicampus church in the Dallas/Fort Worth Metroplex. Since it began in 2000, the church has grown to more than 39,000 active members. His television program is aired in over 190 countries, and his radio feature, *Worship & the Word with Pastor Robert*, airs on radio stations across America. He serves as chancellor of The King's University and is the best-selling author of numerous books, including *The Blessed Life, The God I Never Knew, Truly Free*, and *Frequency*. Robert and his wife, Debbie, have been married 38 years and are blessed with one married daughter, two married sons, and nine grandchildren.

The Blessed Life

ROBERT MORRIS

Too often, greed and materialism can choke out the true spirit of generosity found only in Christ. In this new, revised edition of *The Blessed Life*—featuring fresh stories, illustrations, and testimonials—Robert Morris, founding senior pastor of Gateway Church, examines the true meaning of the blessed life. The enemy wants to keep you from discovering God's principles governing financial stewardship, giving, and blessing. Why? Because once you do, it will change every area of your life from your marriage to your health and finances. It will also impact the kingdom of God.

Book: 978-0-996566-24-7
DVD Message Series: 20150223-DS
Study Guide (Companion to DVD):
978-0-997429-84-8

The Blessed Life resources can be found at the **Gateway Bookstore**.

Did you love using this study guide to dive deeper into *Living in His Presence*? Then check out these other companion study guides by Robert Morris.

ISBN: 978-1-945529-54-2

The Holy Spirit can be misinterpreted as confusing, controversial, and weird.

People often see the Holy Spirit as an "it" and don't believe Him to be a person who can be understood and welcomed.

The Holy Spirit wants to have a relationship with you. These sessions will help you to recognize the Holy Spirit as a person, develop a connection with Him, and embrace His power to walk in a new life.

ISBN: 978-1-945529-56-6

Does your mouth get you into trouble?

The tongue is powerful. Negative or careless words open the door to the enemy and leave a trail of hurt. The good news is words can also be cleansing and encouraging. When used with honor, they can connect us with God and one another!

These sessions will teach you to examine the intentions of your heart, and allow the Holy Spirit to guide what you say.

You can find these study guides at the **Gateway Bookstore.**